To a wonderful
Grandmother …

p

This is a Parragon Publishing Book
This edition published in 2007

Parragon Publishing
Queen Street House
4 Queen Street
Bath BA1 1HE, UK

Copyright © Parragon Books Ltd 2002

This book was created by Magpie Books,
an imprint of Constable & Robinson Ltd.

Designed by Tony and Penny Mills

A copy of the British Library Cataloguing-in-Publication Data
is available from the British Library

Printed in Indonesia

ISBN 978-1-4075-1116-0

INTRODUCTION

Grandmothers today are quite different people from the caricatures of the past. They are just as likely to be found taking aerobic classes or hang gliding or sun bathing in Florida as they are to be making jelly or doing the flower arranging in the local church.

What they have in common with their predecessors is the wisdom and experience they bring to any family crisis or difficulty; the link which they provide to the traditions and history of their own family; and, above all, the encircling love and care which they can give without stinting.

These poems and quotes have been chosen by someone to show they care.

Perfect love sometimes does
not come until
grandchildren are born.
WELSH PROVERB

Grandmothers are the people who take
delight in hearing babies breathing
on the telephone.

ANON

We have become a Grandmother.

MARGARET THATCHER
(4 March 1989)

Grandmothers are good at sitting on the floor
to play,
But they can be terribly difficult to get
upright again.

ANON

Grandmothers have all the fun
and pleasure and pride,
And none of the nappies and tantrums
and sleepless nights.

ANNABEL TWIGG

I have seen many a woman look withered and old in the customary evening-dress which, being unmarried, she thinks necessary to shiver in, who would have appeared fair as a sunshiny October day if she would only have done Nature the justice to assume, in her autumn time, an autumnal livery. If she would only have the sense to believe that grey hair was meant to soften wrinkles and brighten faded cheeks, giving the same effect for which our youthful grandmothers wore powder; that flimsy, light-coloured dresses, fripperied over with trimmings, only suit airy figures and active motions; that a sober-tinted substantial gown and a pretty cap will any day take away ten years from a lady's appearance;—above all, if she would observe this.

DINAH MARIA MULOCK CRAIK (1826—1887)
A Woman's Thoughts About Women

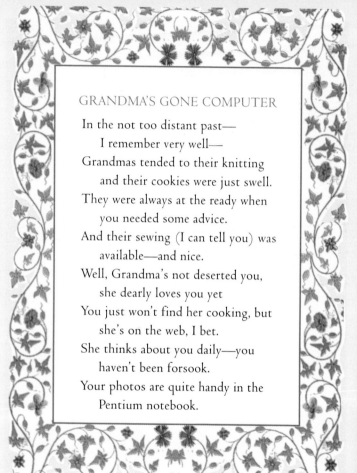

GRANDMA'S GONE COMPUTER

In the not too distant past—
    I remember very well—
Grandmas tended to their knitting
    and their cookies were just swell.
They were always at the ready when
    you needed some advice.
And their sewing (I can tell you) was
    available—and nice.
Well, Grandma's not deserted you,
    she dearly loves you yet
You just won't find her cooking, but
    she's on the web, I bet.
She thinks about you daily—you
    haven't been forsook.
Your photos are quite handy in the
    Pentium notebook.

She's right there when you need her;
　　you really aren't alone,
She's out now with her chat friends,
　　but she took her new cell phone.
You can also leave a message on her
　　answering machine;
Or page her at the fun meet, she's been
　　there since eight fifteen.
Yes, the world's a very different place,
　　there is no doubt of that.
So "E" her on her web page, or page
　　her for a chat.
She's hooked on to the internet and it
　　really seems to suit her.
So don't expect the same old gal, 'cause
　　Grandma's gone "Computer".

PENNY MORRISON

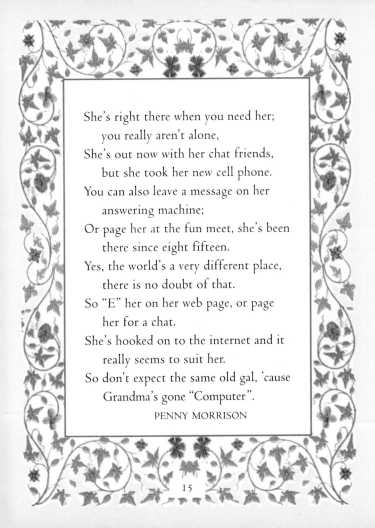

A LONG TIME AGO.

RANDMOTHER

It was a pretty sight to see, however familiar to all of us such things may be—the pale, worn old woman, in her quaint, old-fashioned country dress, holding the little infant on her knees, looking at its open, unspeculative eyes, and talking the little language to it as though it could understand; the father on his knees, kept prisoner by a small, small finger curled round his strong and sinewy one, and gazing at the tiny creature with wondering idolatry; the young mother, fair, pale, and smiling, propped up on pillows in order that she, too, might see the wonderful babe; it was astonishing how the doctor could come and go without being drawn into the admiring vortex, and look at this baby just as if babies came into the world every day.

ELIZABETH GASKELL

from *Sylvia's Lovers*

WHAT IS A GRANDMOTHER?

A grandmother knows everything.
No, not all the little things; she doesn't know the
capital of Ecuador or the square root of sixty-three:

She knows what really matters:
She knows you always mean well;
she knows behind your tears and anger
lie love and kindness more;
She will listen to your troubles and have a lifetime
of wisdom to bring to you;
She will understand your dreams
and pray that they come true;
She has seen her children grow up,
and knows you will do as well;

She knew the best sweets and games to play when
you were small;
She was the first person to know when you had
grown up.

POLLY BRISTOL

Grandchildren love us for ourselves.
They don't try to improve us the way our parents
did; they don't compete like friends;
they don't demand we keep up to date and be less
embarassing as our children did.
They don't expect us to hurry and they don't mind if
we need to sit and rest.
They just love us as we are.

EVELYN HILLS (84 YEARS)

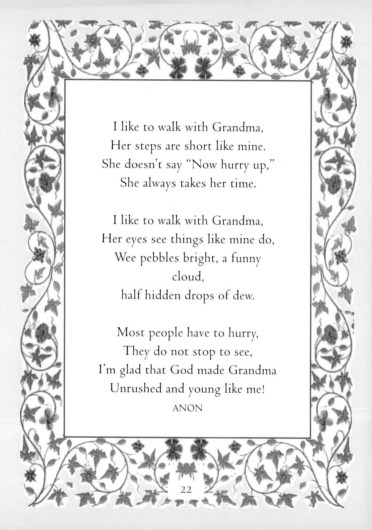

I like to walk with Grandma,
Her steps are short like mine.
She doesn't say "Now hurry up,"
She always takes her time.

I like to walk with Grandma,
Her eyes see things like mine do,
Wee pebbles bright, a funny
cloud,
half hidden drops of dew.

Most people have to hurry,
They do not stop to see,
I'm glad that God made Grandma
Unrushed and young like me!

ANON

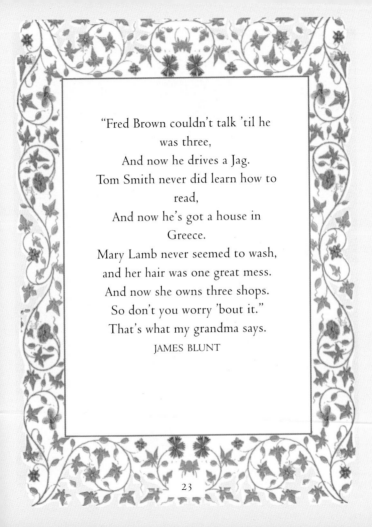

"Fred Brown couldn't talk 'til he
was three,
And now he drives a Jag.
Tom Smith never did learn how to
read,
And now he's got a house in
Greece.
Mary Lamb never seemed to wash,
and her hair was one great mess.
And now she owns three shops.
So don't you worry 'bout it."
That's what my grandma says.

JAMES BLUNT

Went in to see Richard Meredith the Land Surveyor and sat talking to him for some time. He said the old folks used to rise very early, never later than five even in winter, and then the women would get to their spinning or knitting. His grandmother was always at her spinning, knitting or woolcarding by 6 o'clock in the morning.

FRANCIS KILVERT (1840—1879)

Entry from
Kilvert's Diary
Wednesday 19 October 1870

There is a very special chair in our sitting room. Granny gave it to my father when she moved to her bungalow as she didn't have room for all her things. It is very small; made over a hundred years ago, she tells us; made in a time when grandmothers were much smaller than today. It has a pink cover with small red roses and reminds me of the sort of birthday cards old people send to each other.

My mum and dad never sit in the chair, but it stays by the fire to keep warm for when Gran visits, which she does every Sunday when we have a special roast. When I was small I used to find her stories hard to understand but now I love to hear them; not just for themselves but because she wants to tell them and pass on our family history so it stays in my memory as it has in hers. Perhaps one day, I too will sit in the old chair and tell my granchildren tales of long ago when I was young.

EMILY MILES

I wish I could explain to your clear understanding, that I am more annoyed sometimes by your own anxiety to keep the boys quiet and your unceasing attention to them, than by anything they can do—and I would like the girls to be more natural than they are with me and that they should not be lectured too much into pretty behaviour and that if I find a trifling fault and say don't do or do do such a thing that you should neither be offended nor say anything to back me, as if it was necessary. I want not to feel, what I always do, that a daughter in law's children are not the same to me as my daughter's. But till you have sons and daughters with families I do not expect you to think this otherwise than very silly.

LADY STANLEY
from *a Letter to her daughter-in-law*
Mrs Edward Stanley (1844)

Grandmas give you the cherry off the top.

ANON

Grandmothers like to remember:
and to bring to us today
the calm and serenity of another world.

CHARLOTTE WEBB

Grandmothers are meant for kisses and hugs,
For watching rainbows and catching bugs.
For baking all of your favorite things,
For books to read and songs to sing.

ANON

AT
RANDFATHER'S BIRTHDAY PARTY

And the old couple – have they no comfort or enjoyment of existence? See them among their grandchildren and great-grandchildren; how garrulous they are, how they compare one with another, and insist on likenesses which no one else can see; how gently the old lady lectures the girls on points of breeding and decorum, and points the moral by anecdotes of herself in her young days – how the old gentleman chuckles over boyish feats and roguish tricks, and tells long stories of a 'barring-out' [being suspended] achieved at the school he went to: which was very wrong, he tells the boys, and never to be imitated of course, but which he cannot help letting them know was very pleasant too –

especially when he kissed the master's niece. This last, however, is a point on which the old lady is very tender, for she considers it a shocking and indelicate thing to talk about, and always says so whenever it is mentioned, never failing to observe that he ought to be very penitent for having been so sinful. So the old gentleman gets no further, and what the schoolmaster's niece said afterwards (which he is always going to tell) is lost to posterity.

The old couple sit side by side, and the old time seems like yesterday indeed. Looking back upon the path they have traveled, its dust and ashes disappear; the flowers that withered long ago, show brightly again upon its borders, and they grow young once more in the youth of those about them.

CHARLES DICKENS (1812—1870)
'The Old Couple'
from *Sketches by Boz*

Each year my grandma plants six sunflowers in her garden just for me; and in the summer we see how much I've grown. One day, she says, I will be as tall as them and able to look over her fence into the town below.

ALICE PARSONS

I have often wondered how odd it is that my grandchildren think their parents were never young yet they think I understand all the secrets of their hearts.

VERA LOWRY

The curates always came to luncheon at the Rectory on Sundays. They were always compelled to come in ignominiously at the back door, lest they should dirty the entrance: only Mr. Egerton was allowed to come in at the front door, because he was "a gentleman born." How Grannie used to bully the curates! They were expected not to talk at luncheon; if they did they were soon put down ... As soon as the curates had swallowed a proper amount of cold veal, they were called upon to give an account to Mrs. Leycester of all that they had done in the week in the four quarters of the parish—and soundly were they rated if their actions did not correspond with her intentions ...

Generally, however, her real practical kindness and generosity prevented any one minding Mrs. Leycester's severity: it was looked upon as only "her way"; for people were not so tender in those days as they are now, and certainly no servant would have thought of giving up a place which was essentially a good one because they were a little roughly handled by their mistress. In those days servants were as liable to personal chastisement as the children of the house, and would as little have thought of resenting it. Grannie constantly boxed her housemaids' ears,

AUGUSTUS HARE (1792—1834)
Life with Mother

If I had known that grandchildren could be so much fun, I would have had them first.

ANON

Grandmothers just let us be ourselves; and the funny thing is, when we are ourselves it's when we are at our best.

OLIVER KENT

THE NEW

RANDMOTHER

All the old ways of holding a baby, of hushing it to sleep, of tenderly guarding its little limbs from injury, came back, like the habits of her youth, to Bell; and she was never so happy or so easy in her mind, or so sensible and connected in her ideas, as when she had Sylvia's baby in her arms.

ELIZABETH GASKELL

Sylvia's Lovers

When I am sad and down,
my grandma holds my hand;
when I am happy she sits
and smiles with me.
ANNABEL TWIGG

I have six grandchildren and for each I have a
golden charm upon my bracelet. Each night I
look at them and for each I say a loving prayer.
SARAH COLLINS

Grandmothers come
in all shapes and all sizes;
Some are too fat and some are too thin.
Some last all day on a small piece of bread,
While others like wine and quite a large gin.
While the one thing they share, as I have
found out,
Is they're filled full of love, from
without to within.

BRENDA SMALL

44

Grandmothers always buy you *more* sweets
than you asked for.

GERALD YOUNG

Grandmothers have all afternoon to play with
you and never have more important things to
do.

JOANNA FOSTER

Grandmothers can stay awake while grandpa
has his afternoon snooze.

FRED HAWEA

All grandmothers like letters. Even if
they just consist of a squiggle and a
dirty finger mark.

ANON

Yet there is a solitude which old age feels to be as
natural and satisfying as that rest which seems
such an irksomeness to youth, but which gradually
grows into the best blessing of our lives.

DINAH MARIA MULOCK CRAIK (1826—1887)
A Woman's Thoughts About Women

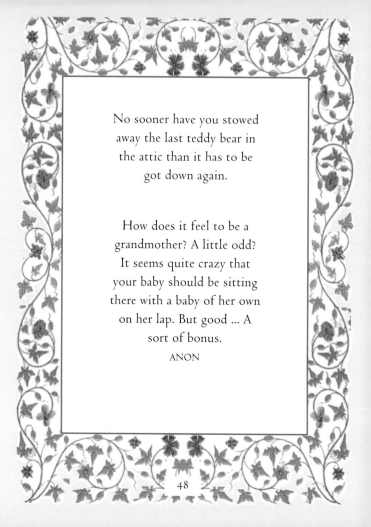

No sooner have you stowed
away the last teddy bear in
the attic than it has to be
got down again.

How does it feel to be a
grandmother? A little odd?
It seems quite crazy that
your baby should be sitting
there with a baby of her own
on her lap. But good ... A
sort of bonus.

ANON

Granny's come to our house,
Ho! my lazy-faisy
All the children round the place
Is ist a-runnin' crazy
Fetched a cake fer little Jake,
And fetched a pie fer Nanny,
And fetched a pear fer all the pack
That runs to kiss their Granny!

Lucy Ellen's in her lap
And Wade and Silas Walker
Both's a-ridin on her foot,
And 'Pollo's on the rocker;
And Marthy's twins, from Aunt Marin's,
And little orphan Annie,
All's a-eatin' ginger bread
And giggle-un at Granny!

JAMES WHITCOMBE RILEY

49

Grandmothers have old feet and young hearts.
ANON

To show a child what has once delighted you,
and rediscover your pleasure in the child's
interest; this is the great happiness
of a Grandmother.
JOYCE MILLER

WHEN WE WENT OUT WITH
GRANDMAMA

When we went out with Grandmama,
  Mama said for a treat—
Oh, dear, how stiff we had to walk
  As we went down the street.

One on each side we had to go,
  And never laugh or loll;
I carried Prim, her Spaniard dog
  And Tom—her parasol.

She said we had no manners,
  If we ever talked or sung;
"You should have seen," said Grandmama
  "*Me* walk when I was young."

She said they never wished then
　　To play—oh, no—indeed;
They learnt to sew or needlework.
　　Or else to write or read.

She told us—oh, so often—
　　How little girls and boys,
In the good days when she was
　　young,
　　Never made any noise.

She said her mother never let
  Her speak a word at meals;
"But now," said Grandmamma, "you'd
  think
    That children's tongues had wheels."

"So fast they go—clack, clack, clack,
  clack
    Now listen well, I pray,
And let me see you both improve
    From what I've said today."
KATE GREENAWAY (1846—1901)

Grandmothers have bottomless handbags.

ANON

Grandmothers have seen it all before and
don't get in a flap.

ANN BERTRAM

Grandchildren are our best compensation
for growing old before we want to.

JANE JACKSON

A CROSS
RANDMOTHER

LADY ISABEL'S carriage continued its way, and deposited her at the residence of Mrs. Levison. Mrs. Levison was nearly eighty years of age, and very severe in speech and manner; or, as Mrs. Vane expressed it, "crabbed." She looked the image of impatience when Isabel entered, with her cap pushed awry as she pulled at her black satin gown, for Mrs. Vane had kept her waiting dinner, and Isabel was keeping her from her tea: and that does not agree with the aged, with their health or their temper.

MRS HENRY WOOD
East Lynne

As I was growing up, I always had the feeling
that I understood a lot more than I knew.
When I listen to my grandchildren,
I think they know a lot more
than they understand.

ANON

I thought I had forgotten how to hold a
baby—but my arms remember.

ANON

When I go to see my daughter and her family,
my grandson shows me all the things he can
play with on his television and his computer, I
can't imagine what wonders his own
grandchildren will have.

ELIZABETH FELLOWES

Grandparents make the world
a little softer,
a little kinder,
a little warmer.

MARTHA WILSON

Being a grandmother is our last chance
to act like a kid
without being accused of being
in our second childhood.

ANON

Grandmas are antique little girls.

OLD SAYING

O Granny please take me to bingo
I could go as your lucky mascot
I think I could pick up the lingo
and I know we'd enjoy it a lot.

You beat me at snap, I admit it
But I'm better at beat the old maid
and the ball goes quite straight when I hit it
and you've often shouted "well played!"

So please take me with you next time.
Think what a good team we'd be.
We could be home before bedtime
so please, Granny, take me.

JOYCE MILLER

Acknowledgments

Jacket picture Grandmother reading to children by Mary Cassatt (1844–1926).
Private Collection, New York, USA/Bridgeman Art Library

page 8 Child Eating Cherries, 1895 (oil on canvas) by Pierre Bonnard (1867–1947).
Private Collection/Bridgeman Art Library. © ADAGP, Paris and DACS London.

page 13 Portrait of Mrs Hearne and her Grand-niece Fanny Sowman by Frederick
Daniel Hardy (1826–1911). Christopher Wood Gallery, London, UK/Bridgeman Art
Library.

page 21 Grandmother and Child, Yorkshire by Henry Silkstone Hopwood
(1860–1914). John Davies Fine Paintings, Stow-on-the-Wold, Glos., UK/Bridgeman
Art Library.

page 24 The Chimney Corner by Joseph Clark (1834–1926). Christopher Wood
Gallery, London, UK/Bridgeman Art Library.

page 28 Posy for Grandma by George Goodwin Kilburne (1839–1924). Fine-Lines
(Fine Art), Warwickshire, UK/Bridgeman Art Library.

page 34 An Evening Story, 1899 by Thomas James R.W.S. Lloyd (1849–1910).
Chris Beetles Ltd., London, UK/Bridgeman Art Library.

page 39 Gran's Treasures, 1866 (oil on canvas) by George Bernard O'Neill
(1828–1917). Guildhall Art Gallery, Corporation of London, UK/Bridgeman Art
Library.

page 42 The Broken Engagement, 1860 (oil on panel) by George Bernard O'Neill
(1828–1917). Private Collection/ Bonhams, London, UK /Bridgeman Art Library.

page 46 Portrait of Auntie, 1922 (oil on canvas) by Lucie Ranvier-Chartier
(1867–1932). Musée Municipal, Billancourt, Boulogne, France/Bridgeman Art
Library. We have been unable to trace the copyright holder of this painting and would
be grateful to receive any information as to their identity.

page 50 The End of the Day, 1868 (oil on canvas) by Hans Thoma (1839–1924).
Hamburg Kunsthalle, Hamburg, Germany/Bridgeman Art Library.

page 56 Granny's Darling, 1861 (oil on hardboard) by Adolphe Tidemand
(1814–76). Coram Foundation, Foundling Museum, London, UK/Bridgeman Art
Library.

page 61 Mother Love by Walter Langley (1852–1922). Christie's Images, London,
UK/Bridgeman Art Library.

The pictures on pages 12, 16, 31 and 40 are by courtesy of Celia Haddon.
All other pictures are from a private collection.